TIANA VON JOHNSON'S

MILLION DOLLAR BRAND™

"And the Lord answered me, and said, Write the vision, and make it plain..." **Habakkuk 2**

BRANDING MANUAL

This Manual Belongs To:

Voureya Shaw

D1469734

Given By:

Message:

Date:

One-Time ONLY Warning

This Material Is Copyright Protected

NOTE: Anyone attempting to repackage, teach, or sell any of this material in any manner whatsoever WILL be pursued!

ALL RIGHTS RESERVED. No part of this book or its associated ancillary materials may be reproduced or transmitted in any form or by any means, electronic or mechanical, including photocopying, recording, or by any informational storage or retrieval system without permission of publisher.

PUBLISHED BY:
Tiana Von Johnson Worldwide, LLC.
30 Wall Street, 8th Fl, New York, NY 10005

DISCLAIMER AND/OR LEGAL NOTICES

While all attempts have been made to verify information provided in this book and its ancillary materials, neither the author nor publisher assumes any responsibility for errors, inaccuracies, or omissions and is not responsible for any financial loss by customer in any matter. Any slights of people or organizations are unintentional. If advice concerning legal, financial, accounting or related matters is needed, the services of a qualified professional should be sought. This book or is associated ancillary materials, including verbal and written training, is not intended for use as a source of legal, financial, or accounting advice. You should be aware of the various laws governing business transactions or other business practices in your particular geographical location.

STANDARD EARNINGS AND INCOME DISCLAIMER

With respect to the reliability, accuracy, timeliness, usefulness, adequacy, completeness, and/or suitability of information provided in this Program, Tiana Von Johnson, Vons World Media, its partners associates, affiliates, consultants, and/or presenters make no warranties, guarantees, representations, or claims of any kind. Participants' results will vary depending on a number of factors, including, but not limited to a Participants' willingness to follow all suggested directions, performing stated actions as often as suggested, and doing all follow-up exercises. Any and all claims or representations as to income earning on this website are not to be considered as average earnings. Testimonials are not representative. All products and services are for educational and informational purposes only. Use caution and seek the advice of qualified professionals. Check with your accountant, attorney, or professional advisor before acting on this or any information. You agree that Tiana Von Johnson is not responsible for the success or failure of your personal, business, or financial decisions relating to any information presented by Tiana Von Johnson, or company products/ services.

While all attempts have been made to verify information provided in this book and its ancillary materials, neither the author or publisher assumes any responsibility for errors, inaccuracies or omissions and is not responsible for any financial loss by customer in any manner. Any slights of people or organizations are unintentional. If advice concerning legal, financial, accounting or related matters is needed, the services of a qualified professional should be sought. This book or its associated ancillary materials, including verbal and written training, is not intended for use as a source of legal, financial or accounting device. The information contained in these written materials and the live training seminar is strictly for educational purpose. Therefore, if you wish to apply ideas contained in these materials and/or seminar training, you are taking full responsibility for your actions. Neither the author, publisher, trainer(s), Tiana Von Johnson, do not, in any manner whatsoever, purport any of the information or materials as a "get rich program" and there is no guarantee or promise, express or implied, that you will earn any money using the strategies, concepts, techniques, exercises and ideas in the materials and/or live seminar training. Earnings potential is entirely dependent on the efforts, skills, and application of the individual person applying all parts of the strategies, concepts, techniques, exercises, and ideas in the materials and/or seminar training. No representation in any part of materials and/or seminar training are guarantees or promises for actual performance. Any statements, strategies, concepts, techniques, exercises, and ideas in the materials and/or seminar training offered are simply opinion or experience, and thus should not be misinterpreted as promises, typical results or guarantees (expressed or implied).

The materials, seminar training and any of its associated ancillary materials and/or trainings are not foruse as a source of professional, financial, accounting, legal, personal or medical advice. You should be aware of the various laws governing business transactions or other business practices in your particular geographical location. The author and publisher disclaim any warranties (express or implied), merchantability, or fitness for any particular purpose. The author and publisher (Tiana Von Johnson or any representative) shall in no way, under any circumstances, be held liable to any party (or third party) for any direct, indirect, punitive, special, incidental or other consequential damages arising directly or indirectly from any use use of materials and/or seminar trainings, which is provided "as is," and without warranties.

PRINTED IN THE UNITED STATES OF AMERICA

© All Rights Reserved. Copyright 2018. Tiana Von Johnson Worldwide, LLC.

HOW TO USE THIS MANUAL

*TAKING NOTES

This manual is designed in a very unique way. You can write notes on the slides pages AND take more specific notes on the notes pages included. The notes page is divided into four unique sections as follows:

- IMPORTANT NOTES - **Fill in the most useful concepts and strategies.**
- WHAT TO APPLY - **Listen for key points of the presentation and outline what you can apply to your business.**
- NEXT STEP ACTIONS - **Outline what you will do in the next 30-days. This is very important for your development.**
- HOW CAN THIS MAKE ME MONEY? **Outline what you will charge, how many units you must sell, etc..... and most importantly, who your client is that will PAY YOU!**

*WATCHING VIDEOS

The videos associated with this presentation are located online.

As you go through the manual, open TianaVonJohnson.com/MasterClassVideos **so can watch the videos that correspond with the slide.**

WARNING!

FOR THE BEST AND MOST EFFECTIVE EXPERIENCE, IF YOU ARE VIEWING THIS MANUAL DURING A LIVE CLASS, PLEASE DO NOT SKIP AHEAD.

CONNECT WITH TIANA

FOLLOW TIANA ON SOCIAL MEDIA @TIANAVONJOHNSON

JOIN TIANA'S EXCLUSIVE VIP EMAIL LIST BY TEXTING "POWER" TO 67463

SUPPORT US! TAKE THIS COURSE AND POST YOUR REVIEW ON SOCIAL MEDIA! TAG TIANA AND USE OFFICIAL HASHTAG #TIANASMASTERCLASS

To Attend a Live Master Class or Webinar, Visit: TianasMasterClass.com

---

To Host a Master Class of 50 People or More in Your City or To Book Dr. Tiana Von Johnson to Speak at Your Next Event, Email Info@TianaVonJohnson.com

---

For Private Coaching or Mastermind Club Rates, Contact: Coaching@TianaVonJohnson.com

TABLE OF CONTENTS

TIANA VON JOHNSON'S

HOW TO BUILD A MULTIMILLION DOLLAR BRAND MASTER CLASS™

LET'S GET STARTED!

TIANA VON JOHNSON'S

HOW TO BUILD A MULTIMILLION DOLLAR BRAND MASTER CLASS™

I AM THE BRAND®

TIANA VON JOHNSON

NO VIDEO RECORDING OF THE SLIDES OR AUDIO RECORDING.

NOTES MANUAL AVAILABLE FOR PURCHASE AT REGISTRATION.

TianasMasterClass.com | TianaVonJohnson.com

Official Hashtag #TianasMasterClass

To Do List
1 Make
2 More
3 Money

AFTER THIS CLASS YOU WILL LEARN:

- ✓ **REAL INFORMATION TO GROW YOUR BUSINESS** NO OTHER SUCCESSFUL ENTREPRENEUR WANTS YOU TO KNOW
- ✓ AT LEAST **5 MORE REVENUE STREAM IDEAS** YOU NEVER THOUGHT TO MAKE YOU MORE MONEY
- ✓ **LOW AND NO COST STRATEGIES** YOU CAN USE TONIGHT TO MAKE YOUR BRAND LOOK HUGE
- ✓ THE 10 BRAND ASSETS YOU NEED TO **TAKE YOUR BUSINESS TO THE NEXT LEVEL** RIGHT AWAY
- ✓ HOW TO LAUNCH A PRODUCT LINE SO YOU CAN **GET PAID WHILE YOU SLEEP**
- ✓ HOW YOU CAN **ATTRACT NEW FREE MONEY** GUARANTEED
- ✓ 15 TIPS TO GET **CELEBRITIES ATTACHED TO YOUR BRAND**
- ✓ A SIMPLE FORMULA TO **MAKE ONE MILLION DOLLARS**
- ✓ 15 MINDSET SHIFTS THAT WILL **CHANGE YOUR LIFE**
- ✓ 10 EASY STEPS TO **WRITE A BOOK IN 2-WEEKS**
- ✓ HOW TO **NETWORK THE RIGHT WAY**

MY 3 PROMISES TO YOU DURING THIS CLASS…

1. Your head will spin with new information and you may say "NOOO, UHHHH, AHHHH… Then your legs may shake and you may start rocking back and forth in awww of the content…
2. You may have a slight headache…
3. You will want to work with me…

TIANA'S 4 BRANDING LAWS™

1. DEFINE Your brand
2. DEVELOP Your brand
3. DELIVER Your brand
4. LIVE Your brand

TO WATCH VIDEO, PLEASE VISIT
TIANAVONJOHNSON.COM/MASTERCLASSVIDEOS

YOUR MINDSET

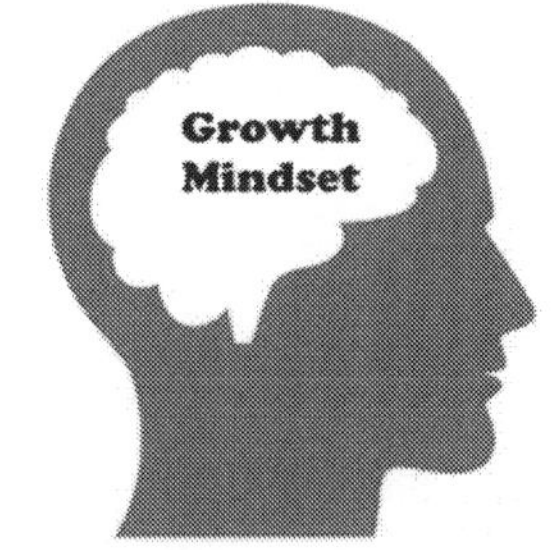

Growth Mindset	Fixed Mindset
I want to learn more. ✓ I use the word invest about my business. I take responsibility I need a coach + mentor. I'm in a business mastermind group. Frustrated → up for the challenge. I am up for the challenge. I am a risk taker. I am going to keep trying If you succeed – I am inspired It doesn't always make sense to voice my opinion.	I know enough. I pay

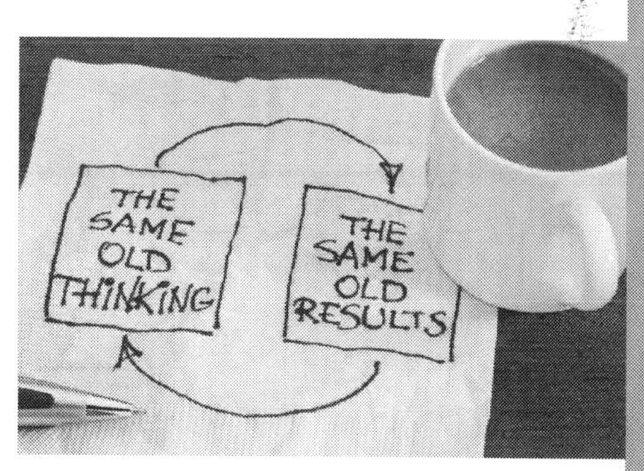

WHAT IS BRANDING?

sounds
tagline
colors
awareness
graphics
design
logo
symbol
BRAND
identity
concept
advertising
marketing
strategic
scents
name
sales
business
consumers

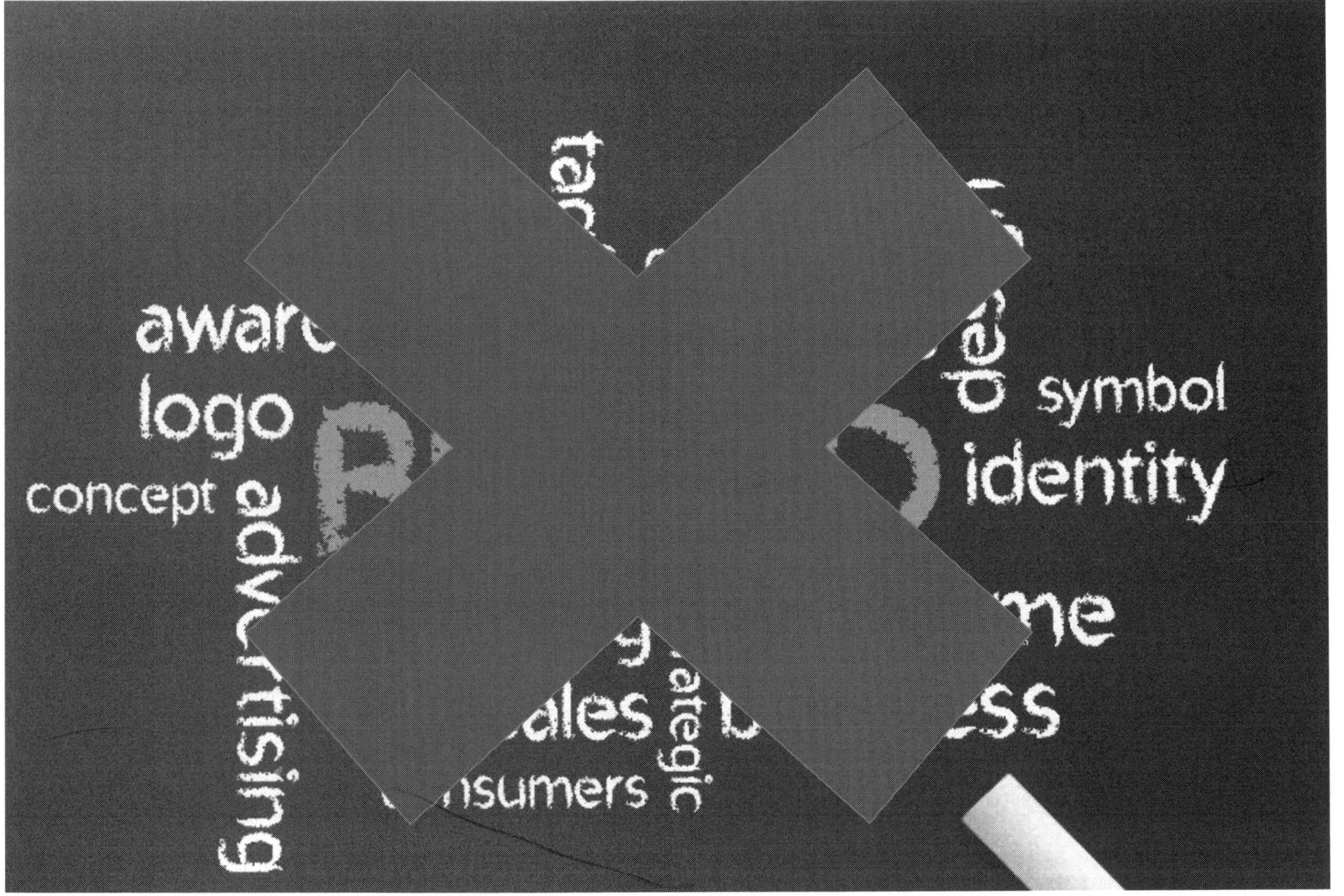
logo
concept
symbol
identity

TOP 3 "CANTS" I HEAR ABOUT BUILDING A MULTIMILLON DOLLAR BRAND

1. I CAN'T AFFORD TO BRAND MYSELF
2. I CAN'T BRAND MYSELF BECAUSE I STILL WORK 9 TO 5
3. I CAN'T BRAND MYSELF BECAUSE I DON'T HAVE A BRAND YET.

WHICH PATH ARE YOU ON?

B-LINE THEORY™

B-LINE TO THE MONEY, HEAD STRAIGHT TO THE BANK!

~Tiana Von Johnson

YOU ARE THE BRAND!

Simply put, your BRAND is about who you want to be and who people perceive you to be.

Who do you want to Be?

- **DO YOU WANT A MILLION DOLLARS OVER THE NEXT 12-24 MONTHS?**
- **DO YOU WANT TO BUILD YOUR CELEBRITY?**
- **DO YOU WANT TO LAUNCH YOUR OWN PRODUCT LINE?**
- **DO YOU WANT TO LIVE THE LIFE YOU WANT?**

WHO IS TIANA VON JOHNSON?

Me, My Tal & Tristen

I'M STILL PRAYING... #FIX IT JESUS!

TIANA VON JOHNSON'S
HOW TO BUILD A MULTIMILLION DOLLAR BRAND MASTER CLASS™

TO WATCH VIDEO, PLEASE VISIT
TIANAVONJOHNSON.COM/MASTERCLASSVIDEOS

IMPORTANT NOTES

What to Apply

Next Step Actions

How can this make me money?

MY STORY

IMPORTANT NOTES

What to Apply

Next Step Actions

How can this make me money?

Where
the magic
happens
...
Your
Comfort
Zone

You are **NOT** in business to run a business!

You are in business to create **FREEDOM** to live the life you want.

WHAT IS SUCCESS TO YOU?

1. Family/Friends
2. Partner/Significant Other/Romance
3. Career
4. Finances
5. Health (emotional/physical/fitness/nutrition/wellbeing)
6. Physical Environment/Home
7. Fun/Recreation/Leisure
8. Personal Growth/Learning/Self-development
9. Spiritual well being (not necessarily religion – can be sense of self)
10. Others could include security, service, leadership, integrity, achievement or community.

WHEEL OF LIFE

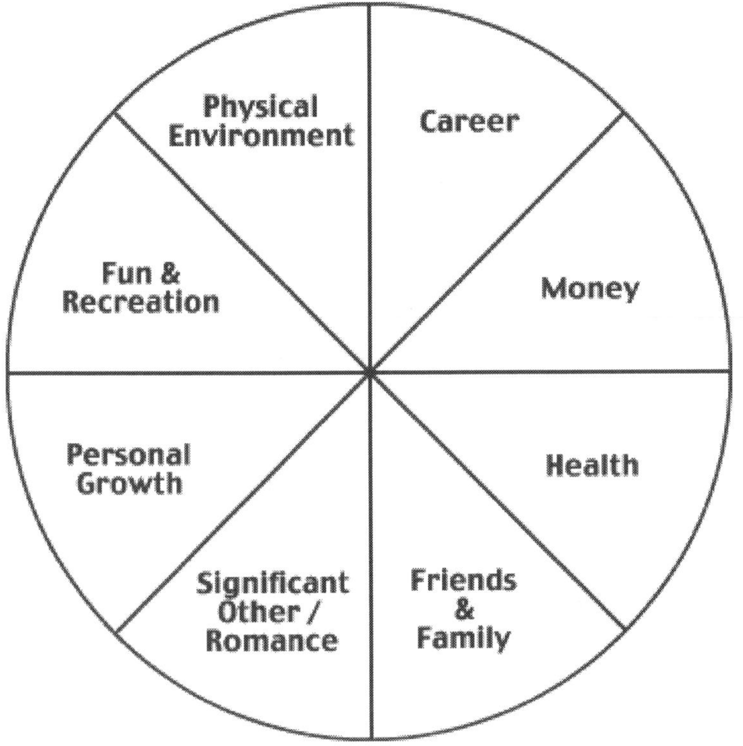

IMPORTANT NOTES

What to Apply

Next Step Actions

How can this make me money?

15 MINDSET SHIFTS

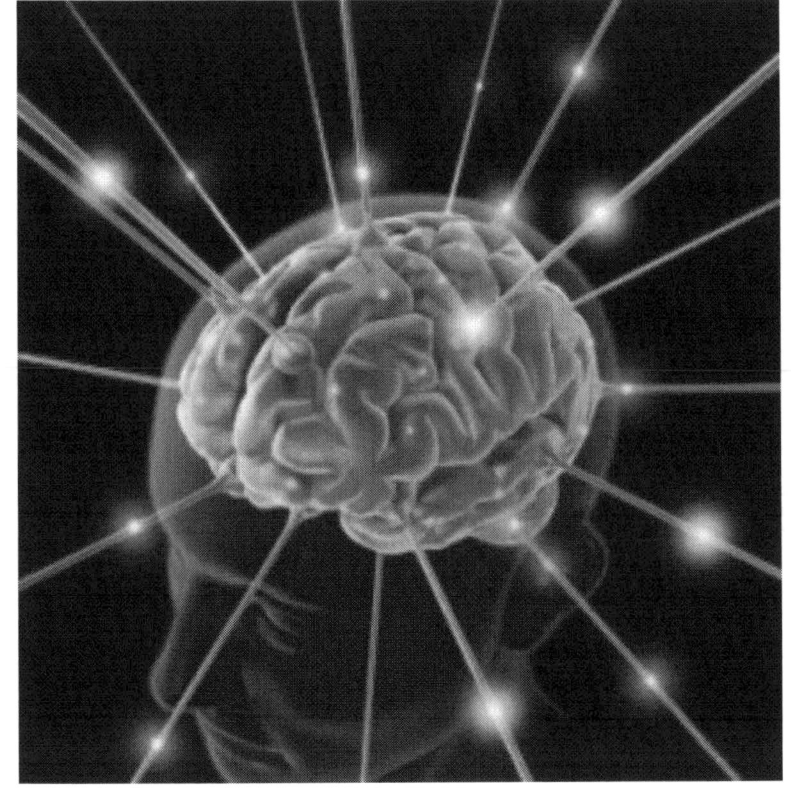

1

START LOVING SALES

2

IT'S NOT ABOUT WHAT YOU MAKE... IT'S ABOUT WHAT YOU RE-INVEST...

3

YOUR DECISIONS DECIDE YOUR WEALTH

4

DEVELOP A STRONG DISLIKE FOR POVERTY

5

DON'T THINK WHAT IF IT DOESN'T WORK... JUST IMAGINE IT WORKING!

6

POVERTY MINDSETS FOCUS ON OBSTACLES, PROSPERITY MINDSETS FIND A SOLUTION!

7

STOP PUTTING MONEY INTO THINGS THAT WILL NOT GROW YOU!

8

JUST GET STARTED AND GET IT DONE! THERE WILL NEVER BE A PERFECT TIME.

9

STOP WAITING FOR:

1. A LOTTO WIN
2. OPPORTUNITY TO COME KNOCKING
3. THE *"IF IT WERE MEANT TO BE"*
4. SOMEONE TO DIE
5. A MIRACLE FROM GOD...

TO BUILD YOUR WEALTH!

"FAITH WITHOUT WORKS IS DEAD"

...NOW GET TO WORK

10

STOP FEEDING YOUR CIRCLE AND LOOK FOR A CIRCLE THAT FEEDS YOU ...AND YOU CAN SERVE.

11

TRY TO NEGOTIATE EVERYTHING BUT STOP LOOKING FOR "A DEAL OR HOOK-UP"

12

NOBODY OWES YOU ANYTHING. YOU HAVE TO GO OUT AND CREATE WHAT YOU WANT!

13

YOU STOP GROWING WHEN YOU STOP LEARNING

14

YOU NEED A COACH WHO HAS BEEN THERE, DONE THAT. EVERY SUCCESSFUL PERSON HAS A COACH!

15

STOP GETTING FINANCIAL ADVICE FROM PEOPLE WHO ARE NOT RICH OR NEVER HAVE BEEN.

BONUS

SIT AT THE FEET OF PEOPLE WITH MONEY AND INVEST IN THEIR BOOKS, COACHING, ETC. DO NOT ASK TO PICK SOMEONE'S BRAIN—IT'S INSULTING!

BONUS

YOU HAVE TO LEARN WHAT TO SELL, WHO YOUR CLIENT IS AND TEACH PEOPLE HOW TO PAY YOU.

BRAND ASSETS

10 BRAND ASSET YOU NEED TO LAUNCH AND/OR GROW YOUR BUSINESS

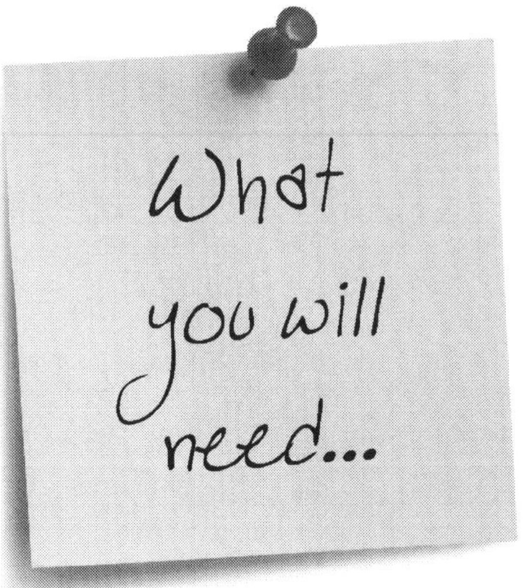

BRAND ASSET 1

Establish your company/brand name. Set up your Corporation or LLC, Get your EIN and your business bank account

BRAND ASSET 2

Get your company domain name via GoDaddy.com for your business AND your personal name you are branding

TIANA VON JOHNSON'S

HOW TO BUILD A MULTIMILLION DOLLAR BRAND MASTER CLASS™

BRAND ASSET 3

STOP USING GMAIL, YAHOO, AOL, ETC.

Set up your new Gmail for business email - yourname@yourdomain.com – info@, jobs@

GMAIL FOR WORK LINK:

http://TinyUrl.com/ChangeYourEmailNow

BRAND ASSET 4

The harder it is for people to reach you directly the better. Create layers, get an Assistant and Setup a secondary phone number

TIANA VON JOHNSON'S
HOW TO BUILD A MULTIMILLION DOLLAR BRAND MASTER CLASS™

BRAND ASSET 5

BRAND STRATEGIST • AUTHOR • ENTREPRENEUR • MOTIVATIONAL SPEAKER • TV PERSONALITY

INTERESTED IN BOOKING TIANA TO TEACH HER *"HOW TO BUILD A MULTIMILLION DOLLAR BRAND MASTERCLASS™"* AT YOUR EVENT?

Dr. Tiana Von Johnson is a serial entrepreneur and world renowned branding expert and strategist for corporations, celebrities and everyday individuals looking to build and develop multimillion dollar brands. In addition, she is a motivational speaker, philanthropist, ambassador-at-large, chaplain, real estate broker, coach and author of the best-selling book *Mindset Makeover*.

Faced with fears and many adversities, she was determined to win and in her first year running her own business she generated over one million dollars. Her Wall Street luxury real estate brokerage, Goldstar Properties and national investment company, Minority Investors Alliance (MIA) was a huge success and she appeared on countless television and media outlets such as TV One, Black Enterprise, CNN, Crains New York Business, Curbed, Marie Claire, News 12, the Real Deal and more. In 2013, she signed a major television deal with NBC Universal for her very own show, *Powerhouse*.

In addition to multiple successful businesses, speaking across the world and television projects, she also runs a private coaching and consulting company where she helps hundreds of entrepreneurs grow their businesses and brand. Tiana teaches her "HOW TO BUILD A MULTIMILLION DOLLAR BRAND & BUSINESS EMPIRE MASTER CLASS" around the world, which is the #1 branding master class in the country.

FEATURES INCLUDE:

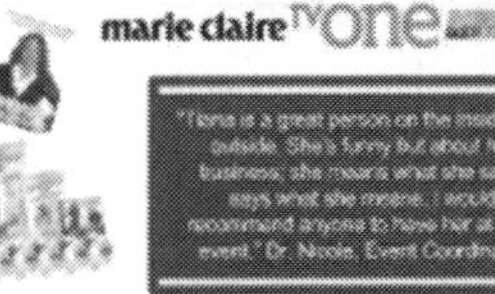

SPEAKING SPECIALTIES INCLUDE:

- HOW TO BUILD A MILLION DOLLAR BRAND
- ENTREPRENEURSHIP & LEADERSHIP
- WOMEN'S EMPOWERMENT & MINISTRY
- BUSINESS & PROFESSIONAL DEVELOPMENT
- REAL ESTATE & INVESTING

FORMATS AVAILABLE TO YOU:

- COACHING & CONSULTING
- LEADERSHIP RETREATS
- WORKSHOPS & SEMINARS
- KEYNOTE PRESENTATIONS
- TEAM BUILDING EVENTS
- BOOKS & HOME STUDY COURSES

"Tiana is a great person on the inside and outside. She's funny but about her business; she means what she says, says what she means. I would recommend anyone to have her at their event." Dr. Nicole, Event Coordinator

BOOK TIANA FOR YOUR NEXT EVENT AS A HOST, GUESTS SPEAKER OR PANELIST
TianaVonJohnson.com | Contact • 866-691-4440 Follow Tiana on Social Media @TianaVonJohnson

BIO

ONE-SHEET

TIANA VON JOHNSON™

ENTREPRENEUR | BRANDING EXPERT | BEAUTY ENTHUSIAST | COACH | SPEAKER | AUTHOR

"B-LINE TO THE MONEY, HEAD STRAIGHT TO THE BANK"

NATURAL LEADER

Dr. Tiana Von Johnson is a million dollar brand strategist, multi-business entrepreneur, motivational speaker, author, publisher and beauty enthusiast. In addition to building her own empires, she helps hundreds of entrepreneurs build their businesses and brands through her personal coaching and mastermind club.

BORN TO WIN

Tiana began her climb to success when she was only seven-years-old. She developed a knack for negotiation and entrepreneurship by selling records on the streets with her father and honed her creative genius by watching her mother do hair, sew, cook, make dolls and design flowers. Combining the entrepreneurial and creative talents of her parents, she became quite a formidable force.

Over the years, Tiana has held various corporate leadership positions in social services and put herself through college. She received her Bachelor's in Business Administration at the age of 20; one year later she completed her Master's in Business Administration both from Metropolitan College of New York and studied for her PhD in Business Administration & Organizational Leadership from the University of Phoenix from 2007-2010. Although Tiana was determined and reached high levels of education and success in the corporate world, she felt this was not her true calling. Miserable with the predictable routine of her day job, the then 27-year-old single mother of two living paycheck to paycheck, Tiana took a step out on faith, quit her job and tried her hand at entrepreneurship.

RISE OF A MOGUL

Faced with fears and many setbacks, Tiana was determined to win and in her first year running her own business she mastered the art of branding and generated over $1 million. Her Wall Street luxury real estate firm, Goldstar and national investment company, Minority Investors Alliance (MIA) was a huge success leading to countless television and media interviews on *TV One, Black Enterprise, CNN, Crain's New York Business, Curbed, Marie Claire, News 12, The Real Deal* and more. In 2013, she signed a major television deal with NBC Universal for her very own show, *Powerhouse*.

EXPANDING AN ENTREPRENEURIAL EMPIRE

Always building brands and on the lookout for creative revenue streams, Tiana realized that she needed to be part of the $72 billion beauty industry. Seeing the high demand for products and services, she launched AMBITION By Tiana Von Johnson, a first of its kind, high-end beauty subscription.

GIVING BACK

Tiana did not want her years of sacrifice, tears, hard work, trials and tribulations to go in vain so she started her coaching program to help other entrepreneurs build their business and brands using her expertise and strategies. In addition, Tiana launched Women Doing It Big (WDIB) in 2012, an organization that motivates and educates women around the world to build their businesses, communities and families through entrepreneurship; her popular signature WDIB Conference is held annually in various cities.

Tiana holds an MBA from Metropolitan College of New York and she was awarded two Honorary Doctor of Philosophy degrees for over 15 years of global business development and philanthropic initiatives nationally and internationally.

FOLLOW TIANA ON SOCIAL MEDIA @TIANAVONJOHNSON AND VISIT TIANAVONJOHNSON.COM

TIANA VON JOHNSON'S

HOW TO BUILD A MULTIMILLION DOLLAR BRAND MASTER CLASS™

BRAND ASSET 6

Design your business AND name logo

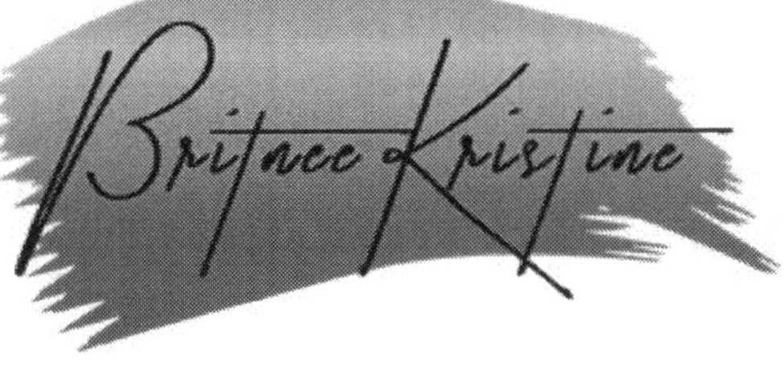

BRAND ASSET 7

fiverr

Anything For $5

TIANA VON JOHNSON'S

HOW TO BUILD A MULTIMILLION DOLLAR BRAND MASTER CLASS™

BRAND ASSET 8

Set up your email blast / newsletter account – Try Mailchimp

START BUILDING YOUR LIST!

Gather ALL email addresses you have and create a list

TIANA VON JOHNSON'S
HOW TO BUILD A MULTIMILLION DOLLAR BRAND MASTER CLASS™

BRAND ASSET 9

Set up your Merchant Account to accept electronic payments

TIANA VON JOHNSON'S

HOW TO BUILD A MULTIMILLION DOLLAR BRAND MASTER CLASS™

BRAND ASSET 10

click funnels

GET A FREE 14-DAY TRIAL

TianaVonJohnson.com/ClickFunnels

TIANA VON JOHNSON'S
HOW TO BUILD A MULTIMILLION DOLLAR BRAND MASTER CLASS™

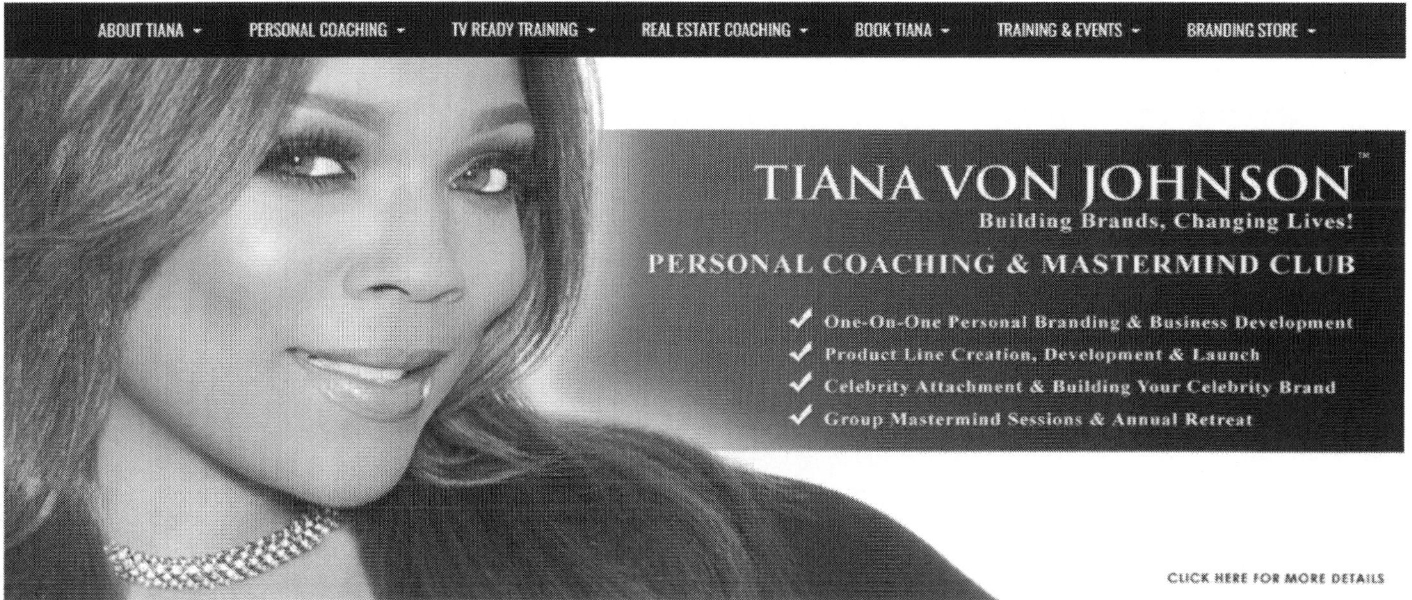

USE POP-UPS ON YOUR WEBSITE
"BUILD YOUR LIST"

IMPORTANT NOTES

What to Apply

Next Step Actions

How can this make me money?

YOUR TEAM

STEVE JOBS SUCCESS SECRETS

TO WATCH VIDEO, PLEASE VISIT
TIANAVONJOHNSON.COM/MASTERCLASSVIDEOS

YOUR TEAM

TO WATCH VIDEO, PLEASE VISIT
TIANAVONJOHNSON.COM/MASTERCLASSVIDEOS

YOUR TEAM

Deliberately seek the company of people who influence you to think and act on building the life you desire.

— *Napoleon Hill* —

TIANA VON JOHNSON'S
HOW TO BUILD A MULTIMILLION DOLLAR BRAND MASTER CLASS™

YOUR TEAM

NAPOLEON HILL
MASTERMIND PRICIPLE

TO WATCH VIDEO, PLEASE VISIT
TIANAVONJOHNSON.COM/MASTERCLASSVIDEOS

IMPORTANT NOTES

What to Apply

Next Step Actions

How can this make me money?

YOUR TEAM

WILL THIS PERSON <u>HELP</u> OR <u>HINDER</u> MY BRAND?

IMPORTANT NOTES

What to Apply

Next Step Actions

How can this make me money?

YOU MUST HAVE THE RIGHT PHOTOS

RE-BRANDING PHOTOSHOOT

RE-BRANDING PHOTOSHOOT

RE-BRANDING PHOTOSHOOT

RE-BRANDING PHOTOSHOOT

RE-BRANDING PHOTOSHOOT

Code30™

RE-BRANDING PHOTOSHOOT

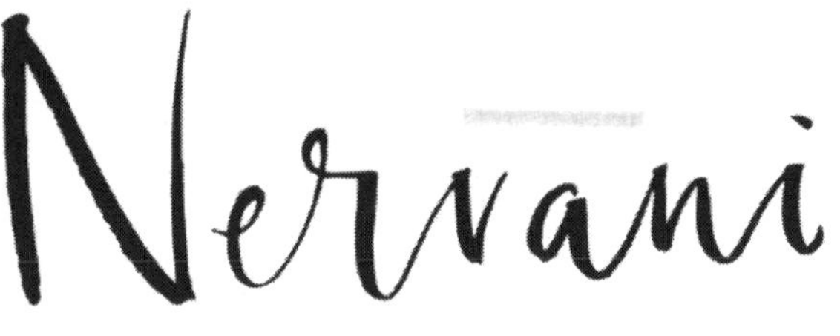

RE-BRANDING PHOTOSHOOT

RE-BRANDING PHOTOSHOOT

NICOLE & NADINE

RE-BRANDING PHOTOSHOOT

RE-BRANDING PHOTOSHOOT

AMBITION™
BY TIANA VON JOHNSON

AMBITION
BY TIANA VON JOHNSON
Attaché
AMBITION
Attaché

IMPORTANT NOTES

What to Apply	Next Step Actions

How can this make me money?

NETWORKING RIGHT

Are you networking right?

NETWORKING

GOAL:

Get something, Get Job leads, Get referrals, Get exposure, Get connections, Get opportunities to grow your business.

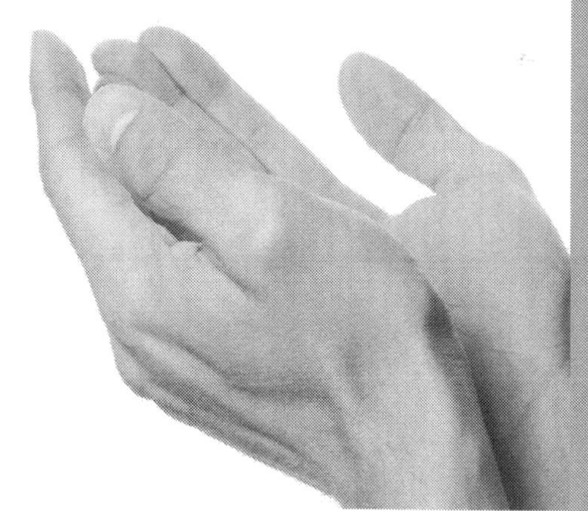

NETWORKING WRONG

GOAL:

Get s ething et Job leads, s, Get exposure nnections, Get o grow y r busi ss.

NETWORKING RIGHT

7 TIPS FOR EFFECTIVE NETWORKING

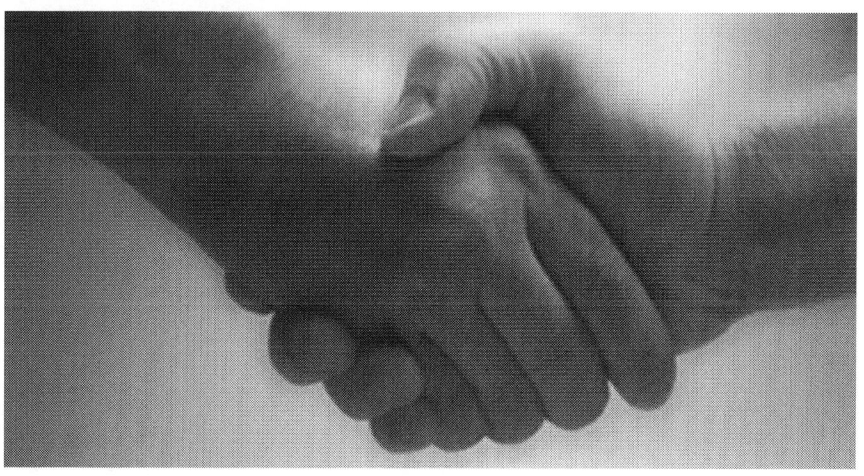

1. **GIVE SOMETHING.** What can you do for someone?
2. **GIVE SOMETHING.** Offer to assist in some way.
3. **FOLLOW-UP**. Send thank you emails or tags and reference one of the points from the conversation.
4. **QUALITY**. Do not focus on Quantity!
5. **DIVERSIFY** your network pool. Travel out to events in other cities.
6. **STOP GIVING OUT BUSINESS CARDS!** Add numbers in your cell phone and send a quick text.
7. **DO NOT GIVE YOUR CARD TO A CELEBRITY OR PERSON OF INFLUENCE** (Use judgement)

NETWORKING WRONG

IMPORTANT NOTES

What to Apply

Next Step Actions

How can this make me money?

NETWORKING WRONG

TO WATCH VIDEO, PLEASE VISIT
TIANAVONJOHNSON.COM/MASTERCLASSVIDEOS

IMPORTANT NOTES

What to Apply

Next Step Actions

How can this make me money?

THE AVERAGE MILLIONAIRE HAS 7 STREAMS OF INCOME

START THINKING IN UNITS

HOW TO MAKE A MILLION DOLLARS

SELL 1 UNIT X $1,000,000 = 1 Million

SELL 10 UNITS X $100,000 = 1 Million

SELL 100 UNITS X $10,000= 1 Million

SELL 1,000 UNITS X $1,000 = 1 Million

SELL 2,000 UNITS X $500 = 1 Million

SELL 4,000 UNITS X $250 = 1 Million

SELL 10,000 UNITS X $100 = 1 Million

SELL 20,000 UNITS X $50 = 1 Million

SELL 100,000 UNITS X $10 = 1 Million

SELL 1,000,000 UNITS X $1 = 1 Million

IMPORTANT NOTES

What to Apply

Next Step Actions

How can this make me money?

WHAT MAKES THESE APPLES DIFFERENT AND UNIQUE?

WHAT DO YOU DO?

IMPORTANT NOTES

What to Apply	Next Step Actions

How can this make me money?

WHAT DO YOU DO?

HOW TO BEST ANSWER THIS QUESTION....

WELL... What is your red apple?
WELL... What are you known for?
WELL... What are the problems you solve?
WELL... What is your creditability?
WELL... What is your story?
WELL... Do you have any testimonials or social proof?

IMPORTANT NOTES

What to Apply	*Next Step Actions*

How can this make me money?

BECOMING A SPEAKER

TIANA VON JOHNSON'S
HOW TO BUILD A MULTIMILLION DOLLAR BRAND MASTER CLASS™

BECOMING A SPEAKER

WHY YOU MUST ADD SPEAKING TO YOUR MULTIMILLION DOLLAR BRAND

1. **YOU GET PAID**
2. **YOU BECOME KNOWN AS AN EXPERT/CELEBRITY**
3. **IT BUILDS YOUR LIST/CONTACTS**
4. **YOU CAN SELL MORE BOOKS/PRODUCTS**
5. **MASSIVE PROMOTION OF YOUR NAME, WEBSITE AND SOCIAL MEDIA**

BECOMING A SPEAKER

TIANA'S SECRET SAUCE

5 KEY TIPS

1. BE FUNNY
2. BE RELATABLE
3. BE LIKABLE
4. TELL YOUR STORY
5. SELL SOMETHING

TIANA VON JOHNSON'S
HOW TO BUILD A MULTIMILLION DOLLAR BRAND MASTER CLASS™

ONE-SHEET

BRAND STRATEGIST • AUTHOR • ENTREPRENEUR • MOTIVATIONAL SPEAKER • TV PERSONALITY

INTERESTED IN BOOKING TIANA TO TEACH HER *"HOW TO BUILD A MULTIMILLION DOLLAR BRAND MASTERCLASS™"* AT YOUR EVENT?

Dr. Tiana Von Johnson is a serial entrepreneur and world renowned branding expert and strategist for corporations, celebrities and everyday individuals looking to build and develop multimillion dollar brands. In addition, she is a motivational speaker, philanthropist, ambassador-at-large, chaplain, real estate broker, coach and author of the best-selling book *Mindset Makeover.*

Faced with fears and many adversities, she was determined to win and in her first year running her own business she generated over one million dollars. Her Wall Street luxury real estate brokerage, Goldstar Properties and national investment company, Minority Investors Alliance (MIA) was a huge success and she appeared on countless television and media outlets such as TV One, Black Enterprise, CNN, Crains New York Business, Curbed, Marie Claire, News 12, the Real Deal and more. In 2013, she signed a major television deal with NBC Universal for her very own show, *Powerhouse.*

In addition to multiple successful businesses, speaking across the world and television projects, she also runs a private coaching and consulting company where she helps hundreds of entrepreneurs grow their businesses and brand. Tiana teaches her "HOW TO BUILD A MULTIMILLION DOLLAR BRAND & BUSINESS EMPIRE MASTER CLASS" around the world, which is the #1 branding master class in the country.

FEATURES INCLUDE:

SPEAKING SPECIALTIES INCLUDE:

- HOW TO BUILD A MILLION DOLLAR BRAND
- ENTREPRENEURSHIP & LEADERSHIP
- WOMEN'S EMPOWERMENT & MINISTRY
- BUSINESS & PROFESSIONAL DEVELOPMENT
- REAL ESTATE & INVESTING

FORMATS AVAILABLE TO YOU:

- COACHING & CONSULTING
- LEADERSHIP RETREATS
- WORKSHOPS & SEMINARS
- KEYNOTE PRESENTATIONS
- TEAM BUILDING EVENTS
- BOOKS & HOME STUDY COURSES

"Tiana is a great person on the inside and outside. She's funny but about her business; she means what she says, says what she means. I would recommend anyone to have her at their event." Dr. Nicole, Event Coordinator

BOOK TIANA FOR YOUR NEXT EVENT AS A HOST, GUESTS SPEAKER OR PANELIST

TianaVonJohnson.com | Contact • 866-691-4440 Follow Tiana on Social Media @TianaVonJohnson

TIANA VON JOHNSON'S

HOW TO BUILD A MULTIMILLION DOLLAR BRAND MASTER CLASS™

ONE-SHEET

HEAR
CHRIS SPEAK

As a positive energy coach, motivational speaker, entrepreneur and mentor, Chris B. Williams captivates with an optimistic outlook on life. Whether working with teens, college students, athletes, organizations or anyone seeking inspiration, he engages and elevates everyone he encounters.

Chris' signature offering within his personal development programs is the highly interactive and most requested workshop:

How to use Positive Energy to Change Your Mindset, Be More Productive and Achieve Ultimate Success!

SERVICES AVAILABLE TO YOU

SPEAKER	COACH
MENTOR	ADVISOR
FACILITATOR	LEADER

Chris has worked with many diverse organizations who have greatly benefitted from his services some include:

"Chris Williams is the best leader I ever coached. He had the character, poise, intelligence and, most importantly, the trust of everyone he played with. I was lucky to coach him in my first year of my head coaching career."
Fran Fraschilla, ESPN

Positivity is a powerful force regardless of your circumstance, through thinking positive and creating positive energy for yourself, you can ultimately change your life!
Chris B. Williams, Positive Energy Coach

TIANA VON JOHNSON'S
HOW TO BUILD A MULTIMILLION DOLLAR BRAND MASTER CLASS™

ONE-SHEET

Neffy is a sought-after speaker, host, moderator and correspondent most known for leaving audiences inspired, motivated, and ready to take action!

SPEAKING TOPICS

Leveraging her background in marketing, broadcast journalism, new media and business Neffy presents and speaks on on topics related to:

- Entrepreneurship
- Personal Branding & Social Media
- Video
- Public Speaking
- Digital Content Creation
- Pop Culture

Book Neffy for your conference, panels, keynotes, private trainings, interviews, profiles, expert commentary and red carpet coverage. Neffy's past and present audiences include college students, corporate teams and staff, entrepreneurs, young professionals, and small businesses.

ABOUT NEFFY

Nefertiti "Neffy" Anderson is a digital correspondent, video producer, and social media strategist who helps entrepreneurs and brands achieve their business goals through multimedia storytelling. Her ability to meet the needs of various target audiences stems from training abroad in Beijing, Hong Kong, Shanghai, and Shenzhen.

Throughout her career at Black Entertainment Television (BET) Neffy interviewed some of your favorite celebrities such as Nick Cannon, K. Michelle, Ciara, Kandi Burress, August Alsina, Diggy Simmons, Keyshia Coles and Nelly to name a few. As the network's social media strategist, Neffy spearheaded the digital campaigns for tier 1 shows and specials such as the BET Awards, 106 & Park and Black Girls Rock.

With 6 years of professional experience spanning television, digital, print, and radio, Neffy balances a career both in front and behind the camera as the creator, producer, and host of her very own show, The Path Less Traveled Series, a web series that exclusively spotlights millennial entrepreneurs.

Named as one of Innov8tiv Magazine's "Top 100 Women Visionary Leaders to Watch," Neffy has been recognized for her work by national outlets such as the American Marketing Association, Z100's Elvis Duran Morning Show, Blavity, Mediabistro and more.In addition, Neffy's global reach and ability to remain relevant in a changing world has allowed her to work with clients such as Adelphi University, Mediabistro and The Jasmine Brand.

TESTIMONIALS

Thank you so much to the beautiful Neffy Anderson for giving a voice to young entrepreneurs!
– Miriam Osei, BCAKENY

You motivate people who want so many things out of their career because you actually have gone out there and got it! – Felicia Singh

Neffy is a talented journalist, changemaker, and the genius behind The Path Less Traveled. You're looking at a cross between Joy Reid and Mama Oprah, with a better curl pattern.
– Jonathan Jackson, Blavity

CONTACT

bookings@neffyanderson.com
neffyanderson.com
@neffyanderson

COACHING

TIANA VON JOHNSON'S

HOW TO BUILD A MULTIMILLION DOLLAR BRAND MASTER CLASS™

IMPORTANT NOTES

What to Apply

Next Step Actions

How can this make me money?

COACHING $

WHAT'S YOUR RATE?

7 KEY TIPS TO GET PAID

1. START CHARGING ASAP & BE REALISTIC
2. ALWAYS OFFER OPTIONS
3. CHARGE WHAT YOU'RE COMFORTABLE QUOTING
4. OVERCOME PRICE OBJECTIVES
5. DON'T WORK FOR HOURLY PAY
6. DON'T GIVE DISCOUNTS BUT CREATE MORE VALUE
7. GIVE BONUSES & SOMETHING FREE

IMPORTANT NOTES

What to Apply

Next Step Actions

How can this make me money?

LIVE EVENTS

EVENTS BECOME A LEAD & SALES FUNNEL

100 X $97 = $9997

IMPORTANT NOTES

What to Apply

Next Step Actions

How can this make me money?

Life map

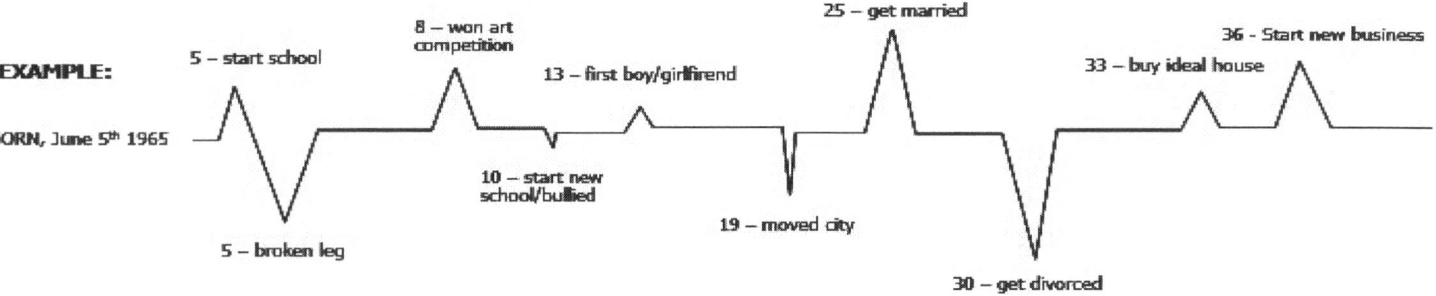
EXAMPLE:
BORN, June 5th 1965
5 – start school
5 – broken leg
8 – won art competition
10 – start new school/bullied
13 – first boy/girlfirend
19 – moved city
25 – get married
30 – get divorced
33 – buy ideal house
36 - Start new business

YOUR LIFE = MONEY
YOUR KNOWLEDGE = MONEY
WRITE LOTS OF BOOKS

Note to self

Write a book, someday

YOU NEED A BOOK TO POSITION YOU AS AN EXPERT!

ANOTHER REVENUE STREAM

SELF-PUBLISHING

Member Order Calculator

Interior Type	Black and Wh ▼	Per Book	Order Subtotal
Trim Size	6" x 9" ▼	**$2.96** each	**$2.96** 1 copies
Number of Pages	175		
Quantity	1		
Calculate			

10 EASY STEPS TO WRITE YOUR BOOK

1. COMMIT TO WRITING THE BOOK
2. THINK OF A COMPELLING TITLE & SUBTITLE
3. PUT THE SKELETON TOGETHER (CHAPTERS)
4. AUDIO RECORD EACH CHAPTER
5. HAVE IT TRANSCRIBED (FIVERR)
6. GET AN EDITOR (FIVERR)
7. SELF PUBLISH (CREATE SPACE)
8. ORDER COPIES (CREATE SPACE)
9. PROMOTE YOUR BOOK/HAVE A SIGNING
10. SELL YOUR BOOK $$$$$$

IMPORTANT NOTES

What to Apply

Next Step Actions

How can this make me money?

SOCIAL MEDIA

CONTENT IS KING!

WHY YOU NEED PROMO AND BEHIND THE SCENES VIDEOS:

1. 89 Million people in the U.S. are going to watch 1.2 billion online videos today and1.5 billion by next year.
2. Online video production will account for more than one-third of all online advertising spending within the next 5 years.
3. More than1billion unique users visit YouTube each month who watch over 6 billion hours of video.
4. 76% of people will add video to their websites, making it a higher priority than other social media platforms.
5. Globally, online video traffic will be 55% of all consumer internet traffic next year.
6. 52% of consumers say that watching product videos makes them more confident in online purchase decisions.

BEHIND THE SCENES

TO WATCH VIDEO, PLEASE VISIT
TIANAVONJOHNSON.COM/MASTERCLASSVIDEOS

GO LIVE

TO WATCH VIDEO, PLEASE VISIT
TIANAVONJOHNSON.COM/MASTERCLASSVIDEOS

PROMO VIDEOS

TO WATCH VIDEO, PLEASE VISIT
TIANAVONJOHNSON.COM/MASTERCLASSVIDEOS

GOING VIRAL!

James Wright Chanel
"The Man Behind the Patti LaBelle's Sweet Potato Pie "

FACT:

ONE VIRAL VIDEO CAN CHANGE YOUR ENTIRE LIFE!

LEVERAGE SOCIAL MEDIA

GOING VIRAL!

EXCLUSIVE: Patti LaBelle Films Holiday Cooking Show with Her Famous Pie Fan: 'He's Like My New Son'

Share on Facebook | Tweet | Pin | +

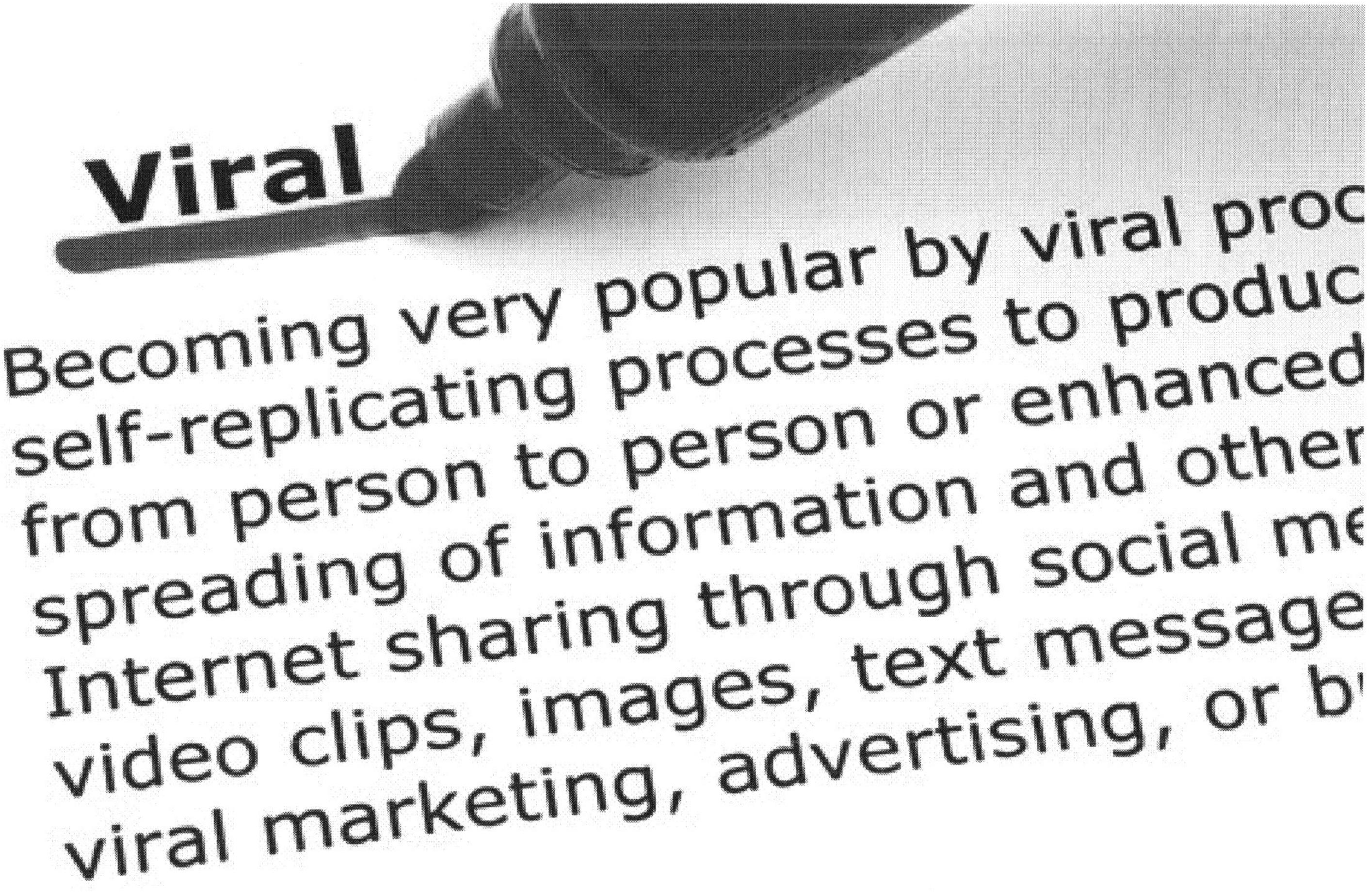

Viral

Becoming very popular by viral proc
self-replicating processes to produc
from person to person or enhanced
spreading of information and other
Internet sharing through social me
video clips, images, text message
viral marketing, advertising, or b

TIANA VON JOHNSON'S

HOW TO BUILD A MULTIMILLION DOLLAR BRAND MASTER CLASS™

TIANA VON JOHNSON'S
HOW TO BUILD A MULTIMILLION DOLLAR BRAND MASTER CLASS™

Cara Hartmann
Known as "The Cat Lady"

TO WATCH VIDEO, PLEASE VISIT
TIANAVONJOHNSON.COM/MASTERCLASSVIDEOS

DO YOU THINK IT'S POSSIBLE FOR ANYONE TO CREATE A MAJOR BRAND?

TIANA VON JOHNSON'S

HOW TO BUILD A MULTIMILLION DOLLAR BRAND MASTER CLASS™

TO WATCH VIDEO, PLEASE VISIT
TIANAVONJOHNSON.COM/MASTERCLASSVIDEOS

TIANA VON JOHNSON'S
HOW TO BUILD A MULTIMILLION DOLLAR BRAND MASTER CLASS™

TO WATCH VIDEO, PLEASE VISIT
TIANAVONJOHNSON.COM/MASTERCLASSVIDEOS

TIANA VON JOHNSON'S
HOW TO BUILD A MULTIMILLION DOLLAR BRAND MASTER CLASS™

TO WATCH VIDEO, PLEASE VISIT
TIANAVONJOHNSON.COM/MASTERCLASSVIDEOS

TIANA VON JOHNSON'S
HOW TO BUILD A MULTIMILLION DOLLAR BRAND MASTER CLASS™

SOCIAL MEDIA

UNDERSCORE

@NICOLE_BROWN

@OFFICIAL_LISA

@IAM_SYLVIAWEST

@DALLASJEWELS_

@KIM_JOHNSON_

SOCIAL MEDIA

REMOVE THE UNDERSCORE

SOCIAL MEDIA

www.blue-shoes.com

www.blue_shoes.com

underscore is hidden

SOCIAL MEDIA

DON'T BE A DIFFERENT PERSON ON SOCIAL SITES. BE <u>YOU</u> ACROSS ALL SITES.

POWER OF SOCIAL MEDIA

WHO IS FOLLOWING YOU?

SOCIAL MEDIA

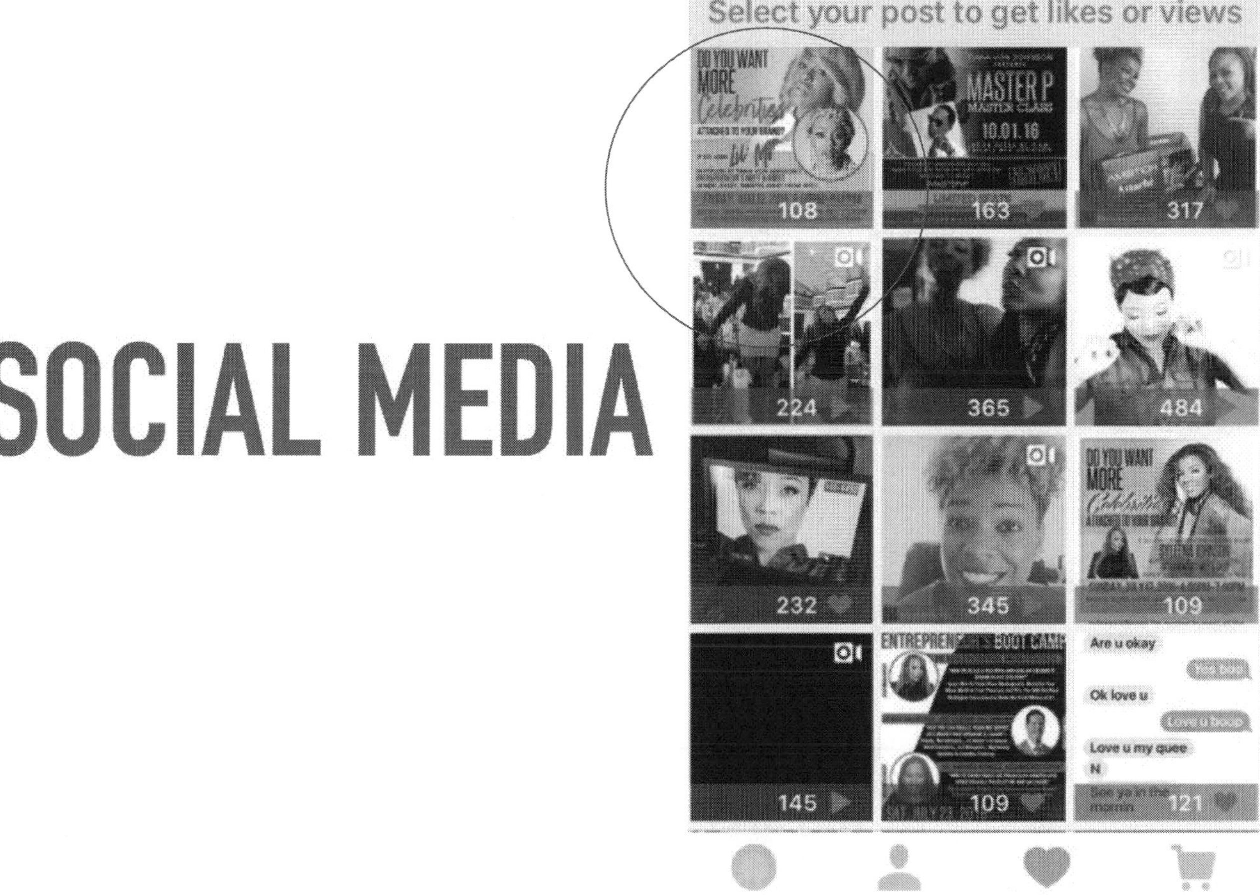

SOCIAL MEDIA

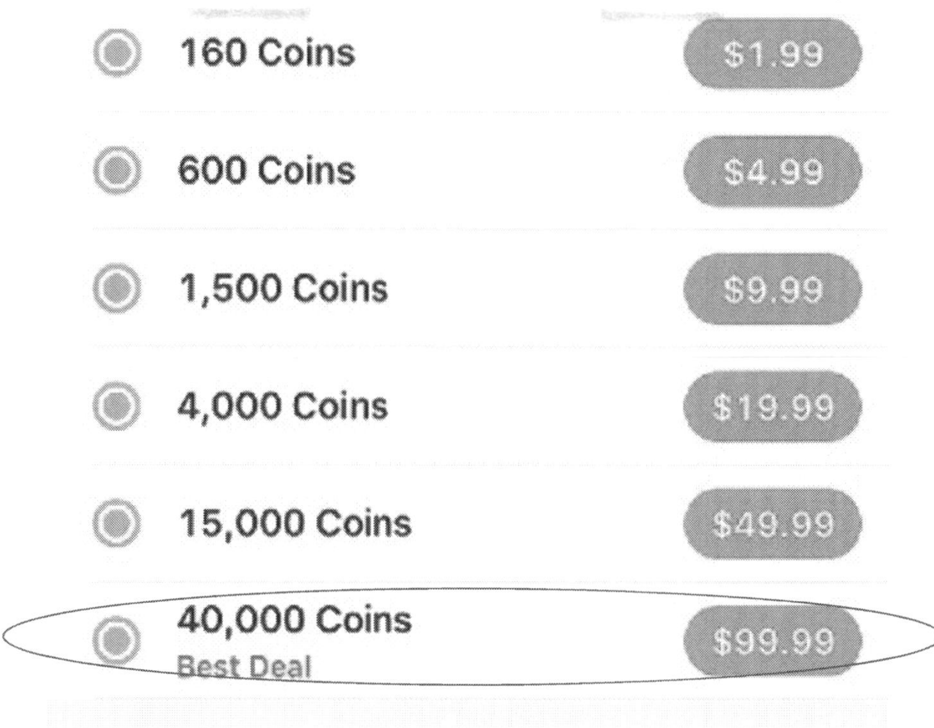

SOCIAL MEDIA

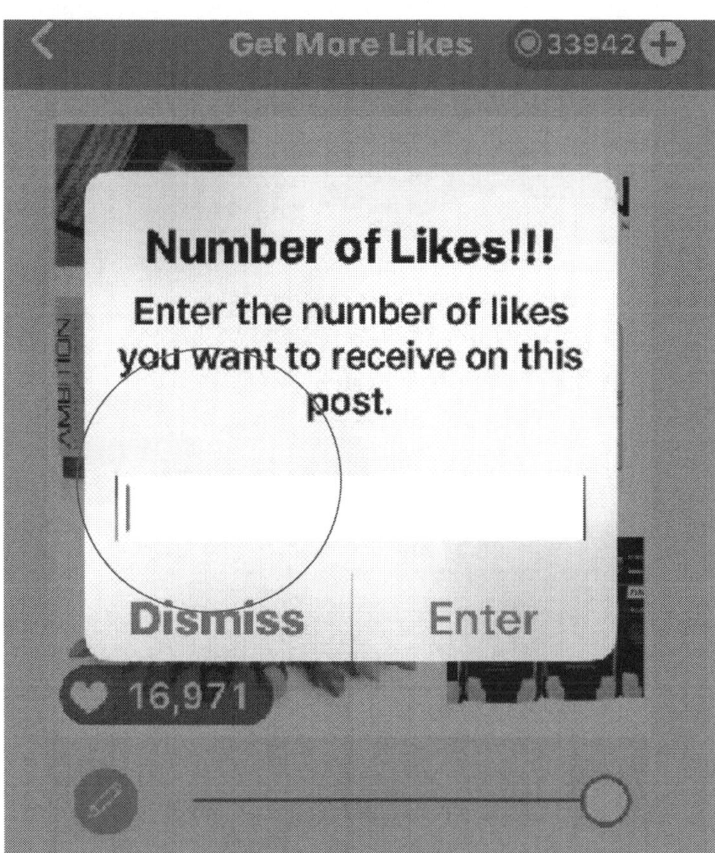

SOCIAL MEDIA

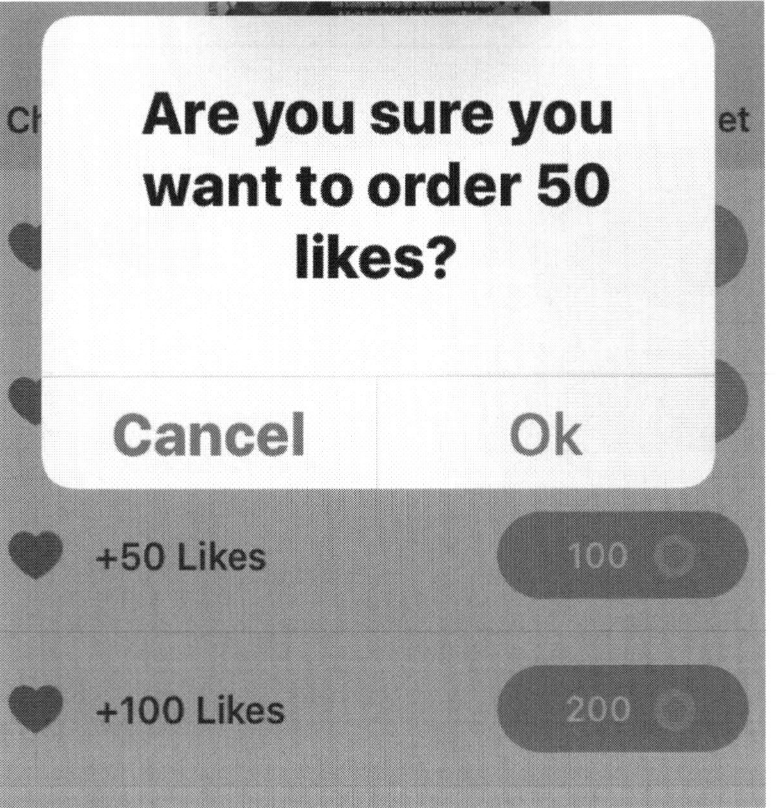

SOCIAL MEDIA

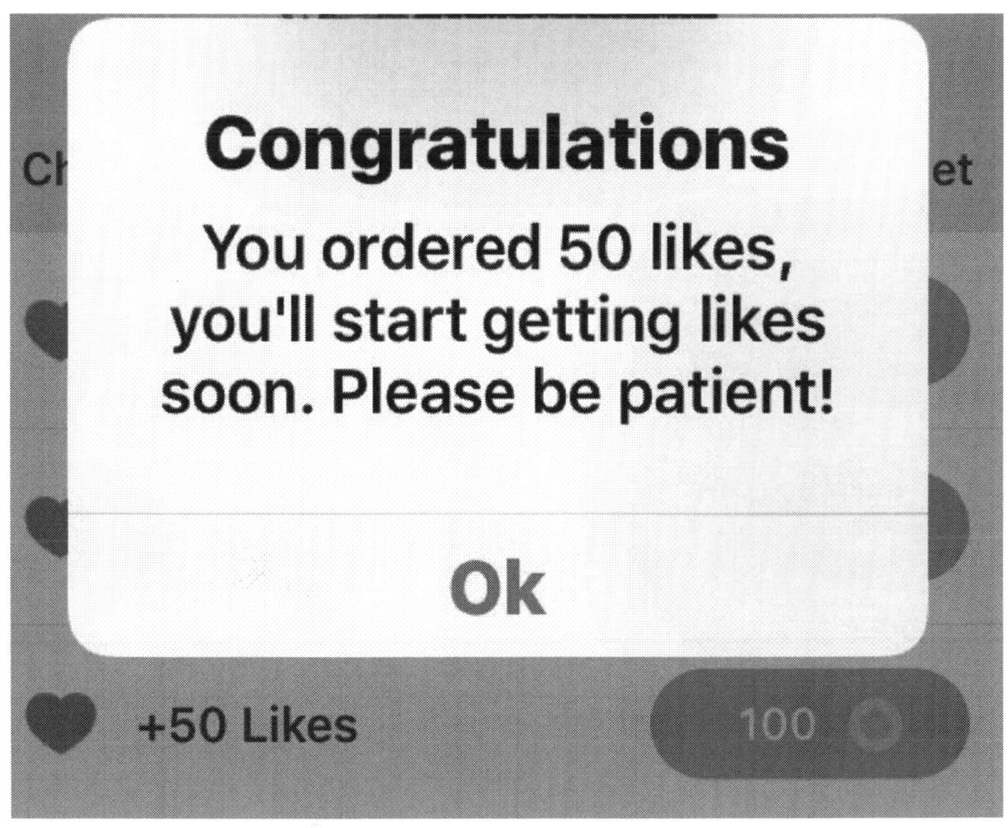

SOCIAL MEDIA

JOIN by TEXT

EXAMPLE:

TEXT "POWER" TO 67463 TO GET
ON TIANA'S VIP EMAIL LIST

SOCIAL MEDIA

REMOVE THE ADS FROM YOUR APPS

SOCIAL MEDIA

REMOVE WWW FROM EVERYTHING!

IMPORTANT NOTES

What to Apply	Next Step Actions

How can this make me money?

CELEBRITY ATTACHMENT

FACT:
IT ONLY TAKES 1 CELEBRITY CONNECTION TO CHANGE YOUR ENTIRE LIFE!

CELEBRITY ATTACHMENT

TIP 1:

JUST START BEING A CELEBRITY

CELEBRITY ATTACHMENT

TIP 2:

ATTACH CELEBRITIES TO YOUR BRAND AND GET AS MANY PHOTOS WITH CELEBS AS YOU CAN

Miss Jessie's
NATURALLY

The MINDSET MAKEOVER
@officialtashera_s

CÎROC

MAKE ME
HAPPY.
WOMEN DOING
IT BIG
ICE CUBE
AMBITION
POWER HOUSE

VON'S
monami
ENTERTAINMENT
MONEY
RESPECT
HAPPY.
myx
MOSCATO

CELEBRITY ATTACHMENT

TIP 3:

USE STRATEGIES THAT THE AVERAGE PERSON WOULD NOT… "THINK OUTSIDE OF THE BOX"

CIRCLE OF SISTERS

moving. changing. growing.

CIRCLE OF SISTERS
moving. changing. growing.

CELEBRITY ATTACHMENT

USE STRATEGIES THAT THE AVERAGE PERSON WOULD NOT… "THINK OUTSIDE OF THE BOX"

CELEBRITY ATTACHMENT

CELEBRITY ATTACHMENT

CELEBRITY ATTACHMENT

CELEBRITY ATTACHMENT

CELEBRITY ATTACHMENT

CELEBRITY ATTACHMENT

CELEBRITY ATTACHMENT

TIP 4:

LET PEOPLE KNOW WHERE YOU ARE ON SOCIAL MEDIA... IN REAL TIME

CELEBRITY ATTACHMENT

TIP 5: HOLD AN EVENT AND BOOK A CELEBRITY

CELEBRITY ATTACHMENT

TIP 6:

ASK CELEBRITIES TO HOLD UP YOUR PRODUCT IN A PICTURE

CELEBRITY ATTACHMENT

ASK CELEBRITIES TO HOLD UP YOUR PRODUCT IN A PICTURE

CELEBRITY ATTACHMENT

ASK CELEBRITIES TO HOLD UP YOUR PRODUCT IN A PICTURE

CELEBRITY ATTACHMENT

ASK CELEBRITIES TO HOLD UP YOUR PRODUCT IN A PICTURE

Derek J

CELEBRITY ATTACHMENT

ASK CELEBRITIES TO HOLD UP YOUR PRODUCT IN A PICTURE

CELEBRITY ATTACHMENT

ASK CELEBRITIES TO HOLD UP YOUR PRODUCT IN A PICTURE

CELEBRITY ATTACHMENT

TIP 7:
TAKE FUN VIDEOS WITH CELEBRITIES

TO WATCH VIDEO, PLEASE VISIT
TIANAVONJOHNSON.COM/MASTERCLASSVIDEOS

CELEBRITY ATTACHMENT

TIP 8:

DO AN INTERVIEW AND MEET-N-GREET AS PART OF THE BOOKING

CELEBRITY ATTACHMENT

DO AN INTERVIEW AND MEET-N-GREET AS PART OF THE BOOKING

CELEBRITY ATTACHMENT

TIP 9:

INVEST IN A SPONSORSHIP AND/OR EXHIBITOR TABLE EVEN IF YOU DON'T HAVE DIRECT ACCESS TO THE CELEBRITY

CELEBRITY ATTACHMENT

FOR IMMEDIATE RELEASE

DR TIANA VON JOHNSON JOINS TARAJI P. HENSON AND A STAR-STUDDED LINE-UP AT WOMEN'S EMPOWERMENT 2017, APRIL 22, 2017 AT RALEIGH'S PNC ARENA

(New York, NY ---April 10, 2017) Dr. Tiana Von Johnson will join a dazzling array of celebrities and guest speakers, including award-winning actress Taraji P. Henson, at the upcoming Women's Empowerment 2017 at the PNC Arena in Raleigh, NC on Saturday, April 22, 2017.

While Henson, who stars as Cookie Lyon on the FOX series "Empire," will give advice on the importance of building a lasting empire, Von Johnson, the CEO of Tiana Von Johnson Worldwide, LLC, will focus on sharing the strategies of running a successful empire.

Celebrating the accomplishments of women while inspiring others to rise to greater heights, Dr. Tiana Von Johnson will present her highly popular Master Class, where entrepreneurs will gain invaluable insight into the inner workings of the business world.

"I am so pleased and honored to be able to appear in such illustrious company at an event that is targeted toward inspiring and enriching the lives of women. I am looking forward to being able to share my knowledge and networking with other women who aspire to have a seat at the table in the business world," Von Johnson commented.

Dr. Von Johnson, a philanthropist, entrepreneur, branding expert, author and publisher, owns a number of successful business enterprises which fall underneath the umbrella of her Bayonne, New Jersey-based company. her Women Doing It Big annual conference, her new publication, Women Doing It Big Magazine, Ambition Beauty Products and the documentary and its accompanying book "Victim To Victory."

The Women's Empowerment & Networking Expo was created in 1995 and formed with the purpose of inspiring, encouraging and educating its attendees. Throughout this expo style event workshops, seminars and lectures are conducted that focus on physical, mental, spiritual, financial and emotional health. The event is being held at the PNC Arena and is sponsored by Radio One of Raleigh and Blue Cross and Blue Shield of North Carolina. CeCe Winans and Hezekiah Walker are part of the star-studded lineup.

For more information about Dr. Tiana Von Johnson, please visit TianaVonJohnson.com or contact XXXXXXX, Email XXXXXX, Phone XXX-XXX-XXXX.

TIP 10:

WRITE A PRESS RELEASE ABOUT "YOURSELF" ATTENDING A CELEBRITY EVENT AND UPLOAD TO PRLOG.ORG

CELEBRITY ATTACHMENT

TIP 11: GET A VIDEO DROP AS PART OF THE BOOKING

TO WATCH VIDEO, PLEASE VISIT
TIANAVONJOHNSON.COM/MASTERCLASSVIDEOS

CELEBRITY ATTACHMENT

GET A VIDEO DROP AS PART OF THE BOOKING

TO WATCH VIDEO, PLEASE VISIT
TIANAVONJOHNSON.COM/MASTERCLASSVIDEOS

CELEBRITY ATTACHMENT

GET A VIDEO DROP AS PART OF THE BOOKING

TO WATCH VIDEO, PLEASE VISIT
TIANAVONJOHNSON.COM/MASTERCLASSVIDEOS

CELEBRITY ATTACHMENT

GET A VIDEO DROP AS PART OF THE BOOKING

TO WATCH VIDEO, PLEASE VISIT
TIANAVONJOHNSON.COM/MASTERCLASSVIDEOS

CELEBRITY ATTACHMENT

BONUS

and....GO ABOVE AND BEYOND TO LEAVE A LASTING IMPRESSION

CELEBRITY ATTACHMENT

BONUS
and....GO
ABOVE AND
BEYOND TO
LEAVE A
LASTING
IMPRESSION

CELEBRITY ATTACHMENT

TIP 12: PARTNER WITH A CELEBRITY ON AN EVENT

CELEBRITY ATTACHMENT

TO WATCH VIDEO, PLEASE VISIT
TIANAVONJOHNSON.COM/MASTERCLASSVIDEOS

CELEBRITY ATTACHMENT

TIP 13: LOOK LIKE A VIP, NOT A GENERAL ADMISSION REGISTRANT

CELEBRITY ATTACHMENT

Celebrity Meet & Greet
FEATURING
SYLEENA JOHNSON

TO WATCH VIDEO, PLEASE VISIT
TIANAVONJOHNSON.COM/MASTERCLASSVIDEOS

TIP 14:

GO WHERE CELEBRITIES ARE AND PAY FOR VIP ACCESS & CELEBRITY MEET-N-GREETS

CELEBRITY ATTACHMENT

TO WATCH VIDEO, PLEASE VISIT
TIANAVONJOHNSON.COM/MASTERCLASSVIDEOS

TIP 15:

GO WHERE CELEBRITIES ARE AND GIVE THEM FREE STUFF!

IMPORTANT NOTES

What to Apply

Next Step Actions

How can this make me money?

LAUNCH A PRODUCT

LAUNCH A PRODUCT

YOUR BRAND CAN REACH MORE PEOPLE BY HAVING A PRODUCT.

LAUNCH A PRODUCT

3 REASONS YOU MUST HAVE A PRODUCT

1. PRODUCTS NEVER SLEEP
2. BUILD YOUR CREDIBILTY
3. MAKE YOUR BRAND LOOK BIG

LAUNCH A PRODUCT

amazon

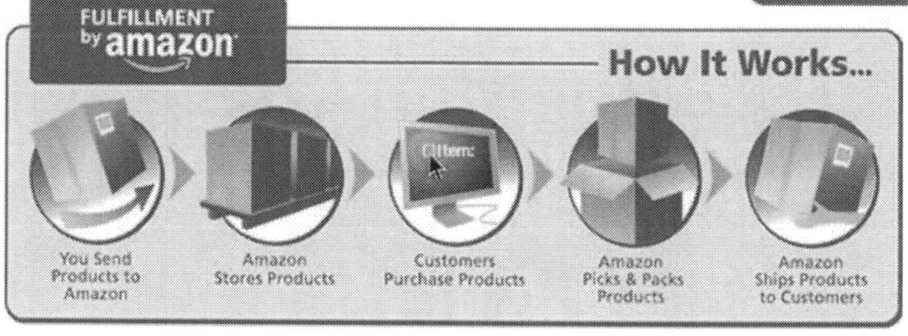

LAUNCH A PRODUCT

PRIVATE LABEL

- HAIR CARE
- COSMETICS
- CLOTHING & SHOES
- FITNESS ENERGY BARS & DRINKS
- FITNESS APPAREL
- FOOD, SAUCES, CONDIMENTS
- FRAGRANCE & NAIL POLISH
- SKIN CARE & BEAUTY PRODUCTS
- TEA, COFFEE & SODA
- WINE & CHAMPAGNE
- CANDLES & HOME DECOR
- PET FOOD & PRODUCTS
- AND MORE..........

IMPORTANT NOTES

What to Apply	*Next Step Actions*

How can this make me money?

LAUNCH A PRODUCT

SELL PRODUCTS ON TV!

The Home Shopping NETWORK sm

IMPORTANT NOTES

What to Apply	Next Step Actions

How can this make me money?

SERIOUS QUESTION....

ARE YOU INTERESTED OR COMMITTED TO BUILDING YOUR MILLION DOLLAR BRAND?

JOIN TIANA'S PRIVATE COACHING & MASTERMIND CLUB

GROUP COACHING IN TIANA'S MASTERMIND CLUB

ANNUAL GROUP MASTERMIND RETREAT

PRIVATE 5-HOUR WORKING SESSION WITH TIANA AT HER HOME

150+ PAGES & CALENDAR

MILLION DOLLAR BRAND VISION JOURNAL & PLANNER™

THIS JOURNAL CAN BE USED IN CONJUNCTION WITH YOUR VISION BOARD OR AS A STANDALONE. YOU CAN COMPLETE THE VARIOUS SECTIONS, USE IT FOR NOTE TAKING AND PASTE COLLAGES ON DIFFERENT PAGES. THE VISION JOURNAL IS A LOT MORE DETAILED AND FUN BECAUSE YOU CAN BE MORE DETAILED AND EXPAND YOUR VISION AND THOUGHTS. I USE MY JOURNAL IN CONJUNCTION WITH MY VISION BOARD TO ELABORATE ON THE THINGS THAT I WANT TO ACHIEVE IN LIFE. SOMETIMES IT HELPS TO DIVIDE YOUR LIFE INTO SECTIONS SUCH AS RELATIONSHIPS, FINANCE, BUSINESS, HEALTH, ETC., SO THAT EACH AREA HAS ITS OWN SECTION AND GOALS.

THIS VISUAL JOURNAL WILL HELP YOU UNCOVER YOUR DEEPEST NEEDS, WANTS AND DESIRES. IT WILL FACILITATE YOUR TRANSITION TOWARD BUILDING YOUR MILLION DOLLAR BRAND. FILL IT WITH NOTES, POWER THOUGHTS, AFFIRMATIONS, GOALS AND IMAGES THAT INSPIRE YOU. TAKE IT WITH YOU TO CONFERENCES, SEMINARS AND EVEN WORSHIP SERVICES FOR NOTE-TAKING. MAKE THIS BOOK PART OF YOUR DAY-TO-DAY LIFE.

ORDER NOW

TianaVonJohnson.com/SHOP

***Inquire about wholesale orders of 25 or more.**

19x25 POSTER

MILLION DOLLAR BRAND VISION BOARD™

A VISION BOARD IS A POWERFUL VISUALIZATION TOOL THAT YOU CAN USE AS INSPIRATION FOR YOUR JOURNEY TOWARD YOUR FUTURE. THIS POWERFUL TOOL SERVES AS A TANGIBLE REPRESENTATION OF WHERE YOU ARE GOING. IT REPRESENTS YOUR DREAMS, YOUR GOALS, AND YOUR IDEAL LIFE. SIT DOWN QUIETLY AND REFLECT ON WHAT IT IS YOU WANT TO ACHIEVE. GO THROUGH MAGAZINES AND OTHER SOURCES TO FIND IMAGES THAT SUPPORT YOUR GOALS. FEEL FREE TO COVER ANYTHING ON THIS BOARD THAT DOES NOT INSPIRE. DECORATE YOUR BOARD, ADD GOALS, COMPLETE THE "TO DO" LIST, FILL OUT YOUR BLANK CHECK AND ADD INSPIRING TEXT UNTIL IT FEELS RIGHT. UPON COMPLETION, HANG YOUR BOARD IN A PROMINENT SPOT. AS TIME GOES BY AND YOUR DREAMS BEGIN TO MANIFEST, LOOK AT THOSE IMAGES THAT REPRESENT YOUR ACHIEVEMENTS AND ACKNOWLEDGE THAT IT IS WORKING. ENJOY THE PROCESS, IT'S MEANT TO GROW YOU!

ORDER NOW

TianaVonJohnson.com/SHOP

***Inquire about wholesale orders of 25 or more.**

100 PIECES

8X10 Full color on thick, durable jigsaw stock with a top coated lamination applied for more durability and resistance.

MILLION DOLLAR BRAND VISION BOARD PUZZLE™

THIS PUZZLE IS PERFECT FOR ANY HOME AND GREAT FOR PEOPLE OF ALL AGES! PLAY ALONE OR WITH YOUR FRIENDS AND FAMILY. ALLOW YOUR CHILDREN TO PLAY AND SEE THE VISION OF THEIR FUTURE COME TO LIFE.

YOU CAN BUY ONE FOR YOUR HOME, AS A GIFT FOR SOMEONE, LEAVE IT OUT ON YOUR COFFEE TABLE, HANG IT IN A PICTURE FRAME OR PURCHASE A FEW AND USE IT AS AN ICEBREAKER ACTIVITY AT YOUR NEXT EVENT.

ORDER NOW
TianaVonJohnson.com/SHOP
***Inquire about wholesale orders of 25 or more.**

IMPORTANT NOTES

What to Apply	Next Step Actions

How can this make me money?

IMPORTANT NOTES

What to Apply

Next Step Actions

How can this make me money?